수적천석 Guide For Teachers & Learners

4차
교정판

[수적천석]은 멘토링/교습에 최적화된 교재입니다.

"고등학교에 올라왔는데 중학교 문법은 완벽하게 잘 숙지가 되어있지 않은 상태로 고등학교 영어에 직면하여 어려움을 겪고 있는" 학생들을 위한 교재이고, (즉 영어 초보 학생들에게 추천하는 교재입니다.)

"영어 수업을 해야하는데, 시중 교재에 마음에 잘 안되는 부분이 있어 고민을 겪고 있는" 선생님들을 위한 교재이기도 합니다.

총 Day 10으로 이루어져 있어 빠른 학습이 가능하며, 이 교재 하나로 단어, 문장 해석, 지문 독해, 문법, 서술형의 기초가 잡히도록 구성하였습니다.

중학교 문법을 빠르게 복습할 수 있는 파트(Day1, Day2), 지문을 읽는 방법(Day3, Day4, Day5), 고등학교 모의고사의 유형 정리(Day6~)로 구성되어있고, 또한 모든 문장과 지문 구성은 고등학교 1학년 모의고사 지문을 발췌해왔기 때문에, 보다 더 효율적인 학습이 가능합니다.

또한 이 교재는 최대한 틀에 박혀있지 않고, 선생님들께서 이 교재에 유동적이고 유연하게 선생님 본인만의 수업을 이끌어 나갈 수 있도록 제작되어 있습니다.

한 파트(Day)를 시작하기 전에, 그 파트에 무슨 단어가 나올 지 점검 할 수 있는 Vocabulary와 한 파트(Day)가 끝나면, 학생들이 스스로 오늘 배운 내용을 점검할 수 있는 과제(Assignment)가 책에 포함되어 있습니다.

학원이나 일대일 과외, 또는 친구들끼리 멘토링을 할 때, [수적천석]으로 기초부터 다질 수 있는 영어 공부를 시작해보는 것은 어떨까요?

*교재 내 오타 및 오류 혹은 기타 컨텐츠 건의: wj0613@kakao.com으로 직접 문의 부탁드립니다.

수적천석 수업 가이드 및 예시
For Teachers

수적천석

발　행 | 2024년 6월 4일
저　자 | 민우준
펴낸이 | 한건희
펴낸곳 | 주식회사 부크크
출판사등록 | 2024.07.15.(제2014-16호)
주　소 | 서울 금천구 가산디지털1로 119, SK트윈타워 A동 305호
전　화 | 1670-8316
이메일 | info@bookk.co.kr

ISBN | 979-11-410-8717-3

www.bookk.co.kr

水滴穿石

수적천석

: 떨어지는 물방울이 돌에 구멍을 낸다는 뜻으로 무슨 일이든지 끈기로 계속
밀고 나간다면 성공한다는 의미.

Contents

Day 1 Vocabulary

- during —(기간) 동안에
- used to —하곤 했었다, (예전엔) —였었다
- provide 제공하다
- movement 움직임, 동작
- public 대중의. 공동의
- transportation 운송 수단
- suburban 교외의, 시외의
- recently 최근에
- discover 발견하다
- mine 광산
- perceive 인지하다, 지각하다
- be likely to-v - 할 것 같다, -할 가능성이 있다
- semester 학기
- diligence 성실함, 꾸준함
- anticipate 예상하다, 기대하다
- outcome 결과
- rate 비율
- rule 지배하다, 통치하다
- genuine 진짜의, 진품의, 참된
- receive 받다
- terrible 끔찍한
- accident 사고
- difference 차이
- attention 집중, 주목
- judgement 판단
- genetic 유전, 유전적인
- track 추적하다, 따라가다
- predict 예측하다
- likelihood 가능성, 가망
- disease 질병
- diagnose 진단하다
- illness 병
- cure 치료하다
- path 경로

- prefer 선호하다
- sufficient 충분한
- respect 측면
- accurate 정확한
- lack 결핍, 부족하다
- common sense 상식
- enormous 풍부한, 막대한
- asset 자산
- literature 문학
- length 길이
- vary 바꾸다, 다양화하다
- intuitive 직관적인
- opportunity 기회
- satisfy 만족시키다
- opposite 반대의
- direction 방향
- deserve (마땅히) -할[받을]만하다, 자격이 있다

Day 1 : 고등 영어의 기초 1(기초 영어 문법을 복습해보자)

#1. 태

1 It was built by King Setthathirath in 1560, during the golden years of the Lan Xang Kingdom.
2-110336

2 Walking to the bus stop <u>used to</u> provide at least some movement, but now most public
1-150338 transportation is limited, so suburban people drive everywhere.

3 One group was paid very well for their time, but the other was only given a small
1-150341 amount of cash.

4 It was recently discovered even 1.3 kilometers below the ground in a South African
1-130330 gold mine.

#2. 시제(완료시제)

5 My wife and I have lived at the Spruce Apartments for the past twelve years.
2-170318

6 If you have been running for 20 minutes, and you perceive it to be only 13 minutes, you're
1-160639 more likely to have seven more minutes of energy.

7 The students had completed their science projects.

8 She had been anticipating a successful outcome on the final exam because of her diligence.

9 This is because the rate of change in Icelandic has always been slow, ever since the
1-150334 country was ruled by Norwegians a thousand years ago and Icelandic history began.

10 Many tickets have been bought by genuine sports fans.
3-080334

11 Early one morning, Donna received a phone call with some terrible news: the younger
1-120343 brother of her best friend, Mary, had been killed in a car accident.

#3. 문장의 형식(2, 5)

12 This difference may seem large, and you might focus your attention on ...(이하 생략)

3-080334

13 we often let emotion affect our judgement.

1-160928

14 This kind of genetic tracking helps doctors to predict the likelihood of a person getting a disease and to diagnose it — although not to cure the illness.

1-160939

15 They seemed like a nice couple.

1-160902

16 Without eustress, you would never get this head to start.
1-160935

17 When Clara had completed the path to freedom, Aunt Rachel watched her get ready to leave.
1-160935

#4 비교급

18 In the 18-34 year-olds group, the percentage of those who prefer red Big/Small City
²³년도 수능 was higher than that of those who preferred Suburb of Big/Small City.

19 As long as you do not run out of copies before completing this process, you will
3-200938 know that you have a sufficient number to go around.

20 Computers can process data accurately at far greater speeds than people can, yet they are
1-200638 limited in many respects — most importantly, they lack common sense.

21 In 2007, hybrid car sales in these three regions were the strongest in the U.S.A.
1-120933

22 It is as difficult as recognizing any new category of objects such as cars and birds.
1-090939

#5 조동사

23
2-140921
Because a great deal of science fiction is rooted in science, it can be used to bring literature out of the English classroom and into the science classroom.

24
2-180943
The third day he tried even harder, but he was only able to bring seven trees.

25
2-140922
I think I may have misled you.

26
1-150637
The cubit sticks must have been very accurate, because the lengths of the sides of the Great Pyramid at Giza vary by only a few centimeters.

#6 강조구문

27 It is the intuitive force that sparks our imaginations and opens pathways to life-changing opportunities.

1-201131

28 This is time-consuming and tiring, no question about it; but it is the only way that satisfies me.

2-100324

29 It is the second train that is moving in the opposite direction.

2-190638

#7 대동사

30
1-160331
I asked if she worked with the airline. She did not, but she deserved the attention, ... (이하 생략)

31
2-170322
I spend more time with my family and friends, and when I do, I am more present

Assignment of Day 1
#배운 문법들을 요약 정리해보자.

#1 태

#2 시제

#3 문장의 형식(2, 5)

#4 비교급

#5 조동사

#6 강조구문

#7 대동사

Day 2 Vocabulary

- comic   만화
- over and over   계속해서, 자꾸만
- womb   자궁
- preference   선호, 더 좋아하는 것
- compete   경쟁하다
- attend   참석하다
- trained   훈련된
- hatch   부화하다
- peck   (부리로) 쪼다, 쪼아먹다
- rely on   -에 의존하다
- nest   둥지
- proper   적절한
- expectation   기대
- consequence   결과, 결말
- certain   정확한, 일정한
- latest   최근의, 최근
- durable   내구성이 있는
- poet   시인
- inspire   영감을 주다, 고무하다
- response   반응, 응답
- otherwise   그렇지 않으면
- propose   제안하다
- policy   정책
- measure   재다. 측정하다
- harmful   해로운
- lie   놓여있다, 놓다
- population   인구
- misguide   잘못 알려주다
- astonish   놀라게 하다, 놀라운
- manage   관리하다
- grateful   고마워하는, 감사하는
- check   수표
- respond   대답하다, 응답하다
- occasionally   가끔, 때때로
- conduct   하다, 수행하다

- moisture   수분
- potential   잠재력 있는
- deceased   사망한, 고인의
- sign   신호
- essential   본질적인, 필수적인
- awareness   의식
- inward   안으로, 속에서
- indentify   알아보다, 식별하다
- context   문맥, 맥락
- related to   -와/에 관련된
- indeed   참으로, 실제로
- stimulant   흥분제, 자극제
- performance   수행 능력, 공연
- suffer   시달리다, 고통받다
- pace   속도
- transformation   변환, 변형
- habit   습관

Day 2: 고등 영어의 기초 2(중 · 고급 영어 문법을 학습해보자)

#1. 관계대명사/관계부사

1 Take your comics with you when you go to visit sick friends who can really use a good laugh.
1- 170328

2 Consider walking which is something that most people do over and over all day long.
1- 140340

3 Once, a friend whom I hadn't talked to in twenty years called me.
1-090333

4 It could hurt her feelings if you tell her what you really think.
1-080327

5 Babies in the womb taste, remember, and form preferences for what Mom has been eating.
1-151141

6 This is where the sound waves coming from moving objects ... (이하 생략)
1-140937

7 Or consider rival holiday parties where people compete to see who will attend their party.
1-200930

8 They became bigger than most trained sea lions in the past, which weren't given enough food.
3-150629

9 After hatching, chickens peck busily for their own food much faster than crows, which rely on the parent bird to bring them food in the nest.
1-180340

#2 준동사

10 The challenge is to find a way to have proper expectations.
1-180629

11 Short press the button to power on / off the device.
2-200328

12 Without an opportunity to experience real-world consequences, kids don't always
1-170923 understand why their parents make certain rules.

13 Getting the latest thing is more important than making durable use of it.
2-110626

#3 분사

14 Discover how world famous English poet William Wordsworth lived, and explore his
inspiring home.
1-180627

15 because it is given as a response to any large flying object, dangerous or otherwise.
1-150930

16
1-181118　Your proposed policy of closing libraries on Mondays as a cost cutting measure could be harmful to these children, ... (이하 생략)

17
1-150930　Hippocrates was the first to understand the physical illness caused by emotional stress.

18
1-111137　Lying 70 km north of the capital city of Stockholm, this city has a population of less than 150,000.

19
1-150930　Misguided, this becomes an obsession, and there is a great difference between ... (이하 생략)

* obsession: 집착

20
1-120924　Astonished, the mother asked her how she managed to do it so quickly.

#4 가정법

21 We would be very grateful if you could agree to this.

1-130623

22 If I were you, I'd call and ask him.

2-150315

23 If the <u>check</u> had been enclosed, would they have responded so quickly?

1-170336

* enclose: 동봉하다

24 So doctors would listen for a heartbeat, or occasionally conduct the famous mirror test to see if there were any signs of moisture from the potential deceased's breath.

1-180939

#5 가주어/가목적어

25 it is essential that we learn to turn our awareness inward and to hear again what our body is always telling us.

_2-190335_

26 It is so important for us to identify context related to information ... (이하 생략)

_1-181120_

27 Indeed, if you have too much of a stimulant, you will become nervous, find it difficult to sleep, and your memory performance will suffer.

_1-220335_

28 The slow pace of transformation also makes it hard to break a bad habit.

_1-200330_

Assignment of Day 2
배운 문법들을 요약 정리해보자.

#1 관계대명사/관계부사

#2 준동사

#3 분사

#4 가정법

#5 가주어/가목적어

Day 3 Vocabulary

- terrifying   무서운, 놀랍게 하는
- scream   비명, 비명을 지르다
- necessarily   꼭, 필연적으로
- preference   선호, 더 좋아하는 것
- immunize   면역시키다, 면역성을 주다
- inject   주입하다, 주사하다
- weaken   약화시키다
- strain   피로, 팽팽함, 긴장
- stimulate   자극하다, 자극을 주다
- develop   개발하다, 발전하다
- antibody   항체
- enable   가능하게 하다
- deal with   -를 다루다, 처리하다
- major   주요한, 전공의. 대다수의
- assault   폭행
- desire   갈망, 욕구
- fulfill   이행하다, 충족시키다
- career   성과, 경력, 직업
- provide   제공하다
- purpose   목적
- reflect   반영하다, 반사하다
- value   가치
- passion   열정
- personality   성격, 개인성
- modern   현대의
- concept   개념
- suggest   제안하다, 암시하다
- burden   짐, 부담, 부담을 주다
- include   포함하다
- unnecessary   불필요한
- instead of   - 대신
- uncertainty   불확실성, 불확실
- miserable   비참한
- interact   상호작용하다
- ranch   농장, 목축장

- cattle   소
- cross-cultural   문화 간
- exchange   교환하다
- offer   제공하다, 제안하다

Day 3: 고등 영어의 기초 3(문장의 본동사를 찾자)

1
1-180619
I let out a terrifying scream that could be heard all the way down the block, but nobody answered!

2
1-150923
Having watched the older children opening their gifts, I already knew that the big gifts were not necessarily the nicest ones.

3
1-140920
When we immunize against a disease, we are in fact injecting a weakened strain of the disease into the body, which is then stimulated to develop the antibodies that enable it to deal with more major assaults later on.

4
1-130334
The desire to have a fulfilling job which is a career that provides a deep sense of purpose, and reflects our values, passions and personality is a modern concept.

5
1-130336
We would suggest that you don't burden your readers with messages that are too long or include unnecessary information.

6
1-091126
Instead of working hard, if one spends time just worrying about the uncertainties of life, he will make life miserable and unsuccessful.

7
2-090932
If you want to interact with people in a country, staying on ranches and cattle farms offers a great opportunity for a cross-cultural exchange and a real experience of life in another country.

Assignment of Day 3

#글을 읽고, 각 문장 마다의 본동사를 찾아 O표 해보자

1
1-081120

Suppose what it would be like to read the story of your life before it actually happens. If you knew how to use the opportunities life gives you, that would really be something. That is the very thing numerology gives you for a happier and more successful life. Now, The Club Prospects, offering you the most wonderful numerology readings, is seeking new members. Just submit your details below and then join our club. You'll share a wonderful journey of discovery with us absolutely free of charge!

2
1-101129

He suddenly found himself lost in a series of monitor control screens as he tried to get back to the main screen. Most systems had a single button or a single command to return to the previous screen or the main menu. But this system did not. After a while, he got the main screen back. He wasn't sure what he had done, but it was back. He paused, looking for a command. Then, he pushed so many different commands. It was no good. He was bothered and couldn't stay calm. For some reason, he was getting consistent error messages. He couldn't understand what they meant. He shook his head in irritation.

3
1-101139

When people work closely together, there are bound to be misunderstandings and communication problems among them. Too much in-person contact might just be annoying, especially if a coworker has a habit we don't like. It is to be expected that people may become impatient with one another if they see each other frequently. Or they may take each other for granted and not make enough effort at communicating properly. Keeping a proper sense of distance between people is important. Indeed, we are likely to get more hurt from being too familiar than from complete ignorance of the other party.

4
1-060629

The summer had passed almost without a single raindrop and once again it was time for the winter farming. Without water, however, there would be no winter farming: no corns, no sweet potatoes, no winter rice. By this time, the Hasari's one remaining cow was nothing but skin and bone. It had been a long time since he had had any straw to give her. She was fed on the leaves of the three banana trees which provided a little shade for his house. One morning Hasari found her lying on her side with her tongue hanging out. It was then that he realized that his other animals were going to die.

5
1-060644

The young people who buy the clothes in the magazines are all fashion victims. They dress in the latest styles and continue to change their image to follow this year's model. While doing this, they are really making a statement about themselves that "Look at me, I have no confidence in my own taste. I want to follow fashion so that other people will not look down on me." So, being fashionable and wearing the latest trends may hide a sense of unease about oneself. Here the clothes are literally covering up the person's sense of insecurity.

Day 4 Vocabulary

- toothbrush   칫솔
- analyze   분석하다
- breath   숨, 숨쉬다
- book   예약하다
- appointment   약속
- detect   감지하다, 인지하다
- lung cancer   폐암
- fascinate   매력적인, 매혹적인, 매혹하다
- connection   연결
- relationship   관계
- gain   얻다
- independence   독립
- renamed   다시 이름 지어진
- imagine   상상하다
- cloudy   흐린, 흐릿한
- blackberry   블랙베리
- bush   덤불, 풀숲
- billions of -   수십억의 -
- struggle   투쟁하다, 몸부림치다
- disorder   무질서한, 장애
- impossible   불가능한
- almost   거의
- mainly   주로
- cause   야기하다, 일으키다
- capable   할 수 있는, 유능한

1 For example, your toothbrush will be capable of analyzing your breath and booking an
1-141130 appointment with your doctor if <u>it</u> detects the smell of lung cancer.

2 Children love animals; <u>they</u> are fascinated by <u>them</u> and can develop very special connections
1-141119 and relationships with <u>them.</u>

3 The farmer chooses two fields and then changes only one thing between <u>them</u>.
1-130635

4 Botswana was once one of the poorest countries in Africa. <u>It</u> used to be called Bechuanaland.
1-130630 After gaining independence from Great Britain in 1966, <u>it</u> was renamed Botswana.

5 Now imagine how well people would respond to you if you showed <u>them</u> that kind of attention.
1-120333

6 Pick up a water bottle, remove the label, and fill <u>it</u> with any water that's not too cloudy from a
1-120330 river or rainwater.

7 Although the salmonberry has thorns, <u>they</u> are much smaller than those of the blackberry or
1-110937 raspberry bush.

8 In fact, billions of people around the world struggle with sleep disorder. For many of <u>them</u>, getting
1-110918 a good night's rest is almost impossible, and <u>it</u> is mainly caused by stress

▌Assignment of Day 4

#it/them 등 대명사를 지칭하는 영어 문장을 5개만 영작해보자.

ex) When I was young, I used to create video games with <u>James</u>. <u>He</u> was kind.
이때 He가 지칭하는 대상은 James이다.

1. _____

_____

위 문장에서_____(이)가 가르키는 대상은 _____(이)다.

2. _____

_____

위 문장에서_____(이)가 가르키는 대상은 _____(이)다.

3. _____

_____

위 문장에서_____(이)가 가르키는 대상은 _____(이)다.

4. _____

_____

위 문장에서_____(이)가 가르키는 대상은 _____(이)다.

5. _____

_____

위 문장에서_____(이)가 가르키는 대상은 _____(이)다.

Day 5 Vocabulary

• depend on	-에 의존하다	• seldom	드물게, 좀 처럼 -않는
• greatly	크게, 대단히	• accept	받아들이다, 수용하다
• fossil fuel	화석 연료	• charge	청구하다, 기소하다
• increase	증가하다, 늘리다	• cost	-비용이 들다, 비용
• carbon dioxide	이산화탄소	• worth	가치, -가치가 있는
• in order to	-하기 위해서	• muscle	근육
• avoid	피하다	• tempting	솔깃한, 유혹하는
• source	원천, 자원	• painful	고통스러운
• solar energy	태양 에너지	• fatigue	피로, 피곤
• produce	생산하다, 만들어내다	• overwork	과로하다
• electricity	전기	• absolutely	전적으로, 확실하게
• aware	인지하는, 알고있는	• likewise	비슷하게
• existence	존재		
• sculptor	조각가		
• on the other hand	반면에		
• research	연구, 연구하다		
• be linked to	-와 연결되어 있다		
• involvement	관여, 개입, 참여		
• be associated with	-와 관계가 있다, -와 관련지어 말하다		
• critical	비판적인		
• verbal	구두의, 언어적인		
• motivation	동기부여, 동기		
• connection	연결		
• confidence	자신감		
• visual	시각적인, 시각의		
• argue	논증하다, 다투다		
• pleasure	즐거움, 기쁨		
• stimulation	자극		
• individual	개인, 개인의		
• according to	-에 따르면		
• foundation	기반, 토대, 설립		
• social bond	사회적 유대감		
• non-profit	비영리의		
• organization	조직		
• entry	입문, 기입		

Day 5: 고등 영어의 기초 5(지문을 읽는 방법을 분석해보자)

01 1-070329

We depend greatly on fossil fuels because about 75% of the energy we use comes from them. The problem is that they increase the amount of carbon dioxide in the air and cause the greenhouse effect. In order to avoid this, we have to find other sources of energy. They have to be clean and less expensive. Scientists think that one such source is solar energy. It can be used to produce electricity, which can then be used to run cars and fly airplanes. Now we should take steps to find clean energy.

02 1-120931

"Art does not solve problems, but makes us aware of their existence," a sculptor once said. Arts education, on the other hand, does solve problems. Years of research show that it is closely linked to almost everything that we say we want for our children. Involvement in the arts is associated with gains in math, reading, critical thinking, and verbal skills. Learning the arts can also improve motivation, concentration, confidence, and teamwork. A report about the visual arts argues that the pleasures and stimulation of the art experience do more than sweeten an individual's life. According to the report, they "can connect people more deeply to the world and open them to new ways of seeing," creating the foundation to build up social bonds.

03 1-120338

What I learned from a man who runs a non-profit organization is "Free advice, free upgrade, and free entry. None are valued." Free advice is seldom wanted. A free upgrade is something you are going to get anyway. Free entry? The band playing tonight must not be any good. People link the value of a service with the amount of money that is exchanged for it. Most people accept that lawyers can charge them $400 an hour. They naturally guess that if it costs an arm and a leg, then it must be worth it.

04 1-120941

If you are looking to improve muscles, it can be very tempting to really push your body beyond its limits. Many people seem to agree that exercise should be painful. But the truth of the matter is that this is a very dangerous idea. Fatigue and pain are your body's ways of saying that it is in danger and is being overworked. While a good workout should offer pressure and challenges, it should absolutely never be painful. Likewise, you should never be pushing your body every day.

Assignment of Day 5

#아래 지문을 읽고 지문을 짧게 요약해보자

1-090634

For many of us, our lives are so filled with responsibilities that it's almost impossible for us to sit still and do nothing — even for a few minutes. A friend of mine said to me, "People are no longer human beings. We should be called human doings." I'd like you to allow yourself to be bored and do nothing. If you allow yourself to be bored, even for an hour, and don't fight it, the feelings of boredom will be replaced with feelings of peace. And after a little practice, you won't feel pressured to be doing something all the time.

요약:

1-090639

Koreans put in the longest work hours among the Organization for Economic Co-operation and Development(OECD) and their work has always been part of Korea's economic success. However, some Korean companies are making an effort to cut back on work hours for their employees. These companies say that giving workers more time to rest has helped their employees to recharge and relax after work, making them suffer less from burnout and be more productive. Their strategies may be working, because these companies record the largest quarterly profit.

요약:

1-090641

On Valentine's Day, millions of people exchange heart-shaped gifts of all kinds, from candy to cards. But did you know that the human heart does not actually look like the typical valentine shape? The human heart resembles the shape and size of a fist. The heart is a muscle with lots of blood supplied to it. In people who are overweight, the heart looks yellow because it is covered with yellow fat. Most people have heard that the heart is on the left side of the chest. In reality, the heart is in the middle of the chest, placed between the two lungs. To push blood, an average heart beats a hundred thousand times a day. It means that in a lifetime, the average human heart will beat more than two and a half billion times.

요약:

In the middle of global economic hardship, many people lose their jobs, pushing the unemployment rate higher. But not all of those fired workers are sitting at home, browsing the want ads and waiting for the phone to ring. Some are heading back to school to equip themselves for a new career, making public colleges and universities among the few bright spots in a poor economy. In fact, some universities in the States are reporting double-digit growth in student registrations this year. University registration managers commonly say that seeing enrollments rise in a failing economy is not unexpected

요약:

In looking for improvements and innovations, we tend to focus our attention on what went wrong. In a typical management meeting, people look at what is not working and try their hardest to come up with ways to put things right. In the process they are often blaming, arguing, becoming negative and getting frustrated. However, if we concentrate too much on what we are poor at, we can easily miss new possibilities. By focusing on our strengths and capabilities, we can create new opportunities. Suppose you have a good voice but can't dance. Then why try to become an all-rounder? Surely it is better to quit the dancing lessons and put all our efforts into becoming a great singer.

요약:

■ Day 6 Vocabulary

• appear	나타나다, 등장하다	
• unsolvable	풀 수가 없는, 푸는 것이 불가능한	
• discuss	의논하다, 토론하다	
• by -ing	-함으로써	
• opinion	의견	
• solution	해결책, 해결방법	
• experiment	실험	
• satisfaction	만족, 만족감	
• introduce	소개하다	
• similar	비슷한, 유사한	
• situation	상황	
• concern	우려, 걱정	
• interact	상호작용하다	
• reduce	줄이다, 감소하다	
• fuel	연료	
• expert	전문가, 고수	
• nutritious	영양가 있는	
• concentrate	집중하다	
• extra	추가의, 특별의, 여분의	
• abroad	해외로, 외부로	
• wherever	어디든지	
• globe	세계, 지구	
• get along with	-와 잘 지내다, 함께 지내다	
• either	어느 한쪽의, 어느 쪽 ..도(..않다)	
• anyhow	어떻게 해서든지, 어쨋든	
• at least	최소, 적어도	
• communicate	의사소통하다	
• realize	깨닫다	
• mostly	주로, 대부분	
• odd	이상한, 기묘한, 홀수의	
• somewhat	다소	
• feature	특징	
• no longer	더이상	
• acquire	얻다	
• through	-통해서	

• mother tongue	모국어	
• environment	환경	
• relative	친척	
• urge	욕구, 재촉하다, 몰아대다	
• express	표현하다	
• be likely to	-할 가능성이 있다	
• unfulfill	미충족의, 채워지지 못하다	
• perhaps	아마도	
• remarkable	주목할 만한	
• conscious	깨닫고 있는, 의식이 있는	
• complex	복잡한	
• code	암호, 약호, 성향	
• patient	환자, 인내심 있는	
• poor	(그럴만한) 여력이 안되는	
• afford	-할 여유가 있다	
• fever	열	
• firewood	장작	
• spare	여분의	
• blanket	담요	
• forehead	이마	
• infected	감연된, 오염된	
• fortuneteller	점쟁이	
• probably	아마도	
• possibly	아마, 혹시, 어쩌면	
• supernatural	초자연적인	
• accuracy	정확도, 정확성	
• based on	-에 기반을 두다[둔]	
• observation	관찰	
• probability	개연성, 확률	
• static	정적인, 고정된	
• astrologer	점성술사	
• palm	손바닥	
• gather	모이다, 집결하다	

Day 6: 영어 모의고사 내신은 어떻게 풀어나가야 하는가 1 (대의파악)

요지, 주제, 제목

01 1-150322

Problems can appear to be unsolvable. We are social animals who need to discuss our problems with others. When we are alone, problems become more serious. By sharing, we can get opinions and find solutions. An experiment was conducted with a group of women who had low satisfaction in life. Some of the women were introduced to others who were in similar situations, and some of the women were left on their own to deal with their concerns. Those who interacted with others reduced their concerns by 55 percent over time, but those who were left on their own showed no improvement.

① 상대방의 의견을 존중하는 자세가 필요하다.
② 대부분의 걱정거리는 시간이 지나면 해결된다.
③ 사람들과 함께 있어도 외로움을 느낄 수 있다.
④ 해결할 수 없는 문제는 빨리 단념하는 것이 좋다.
⑤ 다른 사람들과 문제를 공유하면 해결에 도움이 된다.

02 1-150320

When you skip breakfast, you are like a car trying to run without fuel. Experts say that a nutritious breakfast is the brain's fuel. A brain that is fully fueled concentrates better and solves problems faster. Some students say that getting a few extra minutes of sleep is more important than eating a bowl of oatmeal, but they're wrong. Of course, sleeping is important, but going to bed a halfhour earlier would be better than sleeping late and skipping breakfast. For students who want to do well in school, breakfast is the most important meal of the day. Give your brain the fuel it needs to run well. To think more clearly and faster, eat a good breakfast.

① appropriate sleep time for teenagers
② voods that helps brain activity of students
③ effect of sleep lack on one's studies
④ the importance of breakfast for students
⑤ a desirable learing attitude to achieve good grades

03 1-150620

Have you been abroad? Do you travel a lot? Then you know what I'm talking about. Wherever you go on this globe, you can get along with English. Either most people speak it anyhow, or there is at least somebody around who can communicate in this language. But then, you realize that mostly there's something you may find odd about the way English is used there. If you are abroad, English is likely to be somewhat different from the way you speak it. Well, if you stay there, wherever that is, for a while, you'll get used to this. And if you stay there even longer, you may even pick up some of these features and begin to sound like the locals. What this example teaches us is: English is no longer just "one language."

① pros and cons of travelling abroad
② localization of English in different places
③ necessity for systematic English education
④ various methods to improve English ability
⑤ how to get along with local residents abroad

04 1-150622

Language skills, like any other skills, can be acquired only through practice. In the case of the mother tongue, the child gets sufficient scope for this practice in his daily environment. And he has so many teachers: his parents, other members of the family, friends, relatives — almost everyone with whom he comes in contact in his day-to-day life. He also has the strongest motivation or urge to learn the language, for if he cannot express himself in his mother tongue, some of his basic needs are likely to remain unfulfilled. And what is perhaps most remarkable, the child practices the language without being conscious of the fact that he is learning a highly complex code.

① Who Can We Call the Best Teacher?
② Where Can We Learn Foreign Languages?
③ Why Is Motivation Important in Learning?
④ How Complex Are the Language Structures?
⑤ What Helps the Child Acquire a Mother Tongue?

05 1-150321

Dr. John Ross was well known for helping his patients. Many of his patients were poor farmers, and they could not always afford to pay Dr. Ross's small fee. The good doctor would accept vegetables, eggs, or even a simple "thank you" in payment. One winter afternoon, he went to a house to see a child with a fever. The girl's family had run out of the firewood they needed to keep their tiny house warm. Dr. Ross grabbed a spare blanket from his car and told the father to bathe his daughter's forehead with cool water. Then Dr. Ross left to take care of other patients. After setting a broken leg, delivering a baby, and cleaning an infected finger, he returned to the sick child's house with a load of firewood. He built a fire for the little girl and her family.

* deliver: 출산을 돕다

① A WarmHearted Doctor
② Folk Medicine Really Works
③ The Importance of Family Love
④ A Little Knowledge Is Dangerous
⑤ A Doctor Who Couldn't Cure Himself

06 2-140321

If you've ever visited a fortuneteller you probably came away amazed at the things they knew about you — things no one else could possibly have known. So it must be a supernatural power, right? Research into the fortunetelling business shows that fortunetellers use a technique known as "cold reading," which can produce an accuracy of around 80 percent when "reading" a person you've never met. While it can appear magical to some people, it is simply a process based on the careful observation of bodylanguage signals plus an understanding of human nature and a knowledge of probability statistics. It's a technique practiced by tarot card readers, astrologers, and palm readers to gather information about a "client."

① Don't Ignore Supernatural Things
② How FortuneTellers Know So Much
③ Why People Want Their Fortune Told
④ Non-verbal Signals Show Your Emotions
⑤ Your Future Depends on Your Willpower

Assignment of Day 6

01 다음 글의 요지로 가장 적절한 것은? 1-150919

You've probably looked around you and noticed that all people are unique and different. Even people who might seem really similar in certain ways can also be very different. From different appearances, to different personalities, to different beliefs — it's a big world full of interesting and diverse people! It is tolerance that protects the diversity which makes the world so exciting. Tolerance is the idea that all people should be equally accepted and equally treated, regardless of their differences from others. It's a lot like fairness. Having tolerance means giving every person the same consideration, despite a person's opinions, background, appearance, or other qualities, and whether or not those things are the same as your own. Tolerance allows the world to flourish. That is why treating other people with tolerance is very important.

① 긍정적인 사고방식은 삶의 가치를 높인다.
② 다양성을 수용하는 관용적인 태도가 필요하다.
③ 의사 결정 시 공과 사를 엄격히 구분해야 한다.
④ 타인의 실수에 대해 용서하는 마음을 가져야 한다.
⑤ 객관적 근거를 바탕으로 자신의 의견을 주장해야 한다.

02 다음 글의 요지로 가장 적절한 것은? 1-160321

It is important to recognize your pet's particular needs and respect them. If your pet is an athletic, highenergy dog, for example, he or she is going to be much more manageable indoors if you take him or her outside to chase a ball for an hour every day. If your cat is shy and timid, he or she won't want to be dressed up and displayed in cat shows. Similarly, you cannot expect macaws to be quiet and still all the time — they are, by nature, loud and emotional creatures, and it is not their fault that your apartment doesn't absorb sound as well as a rain forest.

* macaw: 마코 앵무새

① 애완동물에게는 적절한 운동이 필요하다.
② 애완동물도 다양한 감정을 느낄 수 있다.
③ 애완동물의 개별적 특성을 존중해야 한다.
④ 자신의 상황에 맞는 애완동물을 선택해야 한다.
⑤ 훈련을 통해 애완동물의 행동을 교정할 수 있다.

03 다음 글의 요지로 가장 적절한 것은? 1-170320

Recent studies show some interesting findings about habit formation. In these studies, students who successfully acquired one positive habit reported less stress; less impulsive spending; better dietary habits; decreased caffeine consumption; fewer hours spent watching TV; and even fewer dirty dishes. Keep working on one habit long enough, and not only does it become easier, but so do other things as well. It's why those with the right habits seem to do better than others. They're doing the most important thing regularly and, as a result, everything else is easier.

① 참을성이 많을수록 성공할 가능성이 커진다.
② 한 번 들인 나쁜 습관은 쉽게 고쳐지지 않는다.
③ 나이가 들어갈수록 좋은 습관을 형성하기 힘들다.
④ 무리한 목표를 세우면 달성하지 못할 가능성이 크다.
⑤ 하나의 좋은 습관 형성은 생활 전반에 긍정적 효과가 있다.

04 다음 글의 주제로 가장 적절한 것은? 1-150921

Science fiction involves much more than shiny robots and fantastical spaceships. In fact, many of the most outlandish pieces of science fiction have their basis in scientific facts. Because a great deal of science fiction is rooted in science, it can be used to bring literature out of the English classroom and into the science classroom. Not only does science fiction help students see scientific principles in action, but it also builds their critical thinking and creative skills. As students read a science fiction text, they must connect the text with the scientific principles they have learned. Students can read a science fiction text and a non-fiction text covering similar ideas and compare and contrast the two. Students can also build their creative skills by seeing scientific principles used in a different way, possibly creating science fiction stories of their own or imagining new ways to apply the knowledge and skills they have learned.

* outlandish: 이상한, 기이한

① common themes in science fiction movies
② influence of science fiction on popular culture
③ examples of scientific principles in science fiction
④ historical development of the science fiction genre
⑤ benefits of using science fiction in the science classroom

If you're all focused on the game, no matter how much time passes, you'll just focus on the game. So when you're playing, all outside activities will be blocked. For example, you probably won't hear your friend call you, you won't hear your phone call, and of course you don't even know what time it is. In other words, when a person is focused in something, all senses are focused on that immersion, so they don't have the energy to focus on other situations. So if you want to move away from the distraction, try to focus on something. Then, the same principle as above will focus all your attention on immersion, regardless of whether you're immersed in something, so naturally your distraction will decrease.

① advantages of developing informatization knowledge for social communication
② necessity of playing video games to make easier people to do their tasks immediately
③ importance of concentrating to improve your gaming ability
④ powerful method to remove your distraction by focusing on something
⑤ examples of enhancing your concentration skills

One day after the space shuttle Challenger exploded, Ulric Neisser asked a class of 106 students to write down exactly where they were when they heard the news. Two and a half years later, he asked them the same question. In that second interview, 25 percent of the students gave completely different accounts of where they were. Half had significant errors in their answers and less than 10 percent remembered with any real accuracy. Results such as these are part of the reason people make mistakes on the witness stand when they are asked months later to describe a crime they witnessed. Between 1989 and 2007, 2011 prisoners in the United States were proven innocent on the basis of DNA evidence. Seventy-five percent of those prisoners had been declared guilty on the basis of mistaken eyewitness accounts.

① causes of major space mission failures
② inaccuracy of information recalled over time
③ importance of protecting witnesses from threats
④ factors that improve people's longterm memories
⑤ ways to collect DNA evidence in crime investigations

07 다음 글의 주제로 가장 적절한 것은? 1-170321

Noise in the classroom has negative effects on communication patterns and the ability to pay attention. Thus, it is not surprising that constant exposure to noise is related to children's academic achievement, particularly in its negative effects on reading and learning to read. Some researchers found that, when preschool classrooms were changed to reduce noise levels, the children spoke to each other more often and in more complete sentences, and their performance on prereading tests improved. Research with older children suggests similar findings. On reading and math tests, elementary and high school students in noisy schools or classrooms consistently perform below those in quieter settings.

① impacts of noise on academic achievement
② new trends in classroom design
③ ways to control a noisy class
④ various kinds of reading activities
⑤ roles of reading in improving writing skills

08 다음 글의 제목으로 가장 적절한 것은? 1-150922

Consider an innocent question asked years ago by a son to his father: "Who invented the automobile?" Trying to be instructive, the father told his son that in about 1886 Karl Benz invented the automobile. "Wow, he must have been a real genius to figure out the engine, the brakes, the spark plugs, the wheels, and how everything worked together!" "Well, someone else invented the tires; I think it was Firestone. And then there was even the person who invented the wheel...." But then he experienced a moment of realization. "I think I may have misled you. No one person invented all of the components of the automobile. Many people made significant discoveries that led to the invention of the automobile."

① The Trap of Group Thinking
② Curiosity: A Key to Success
③ Always Think About What's Next
④ More Successes, More Good Ideas
⑤ One Great Invention, Many Inventors

09 다음 글의 제목으로 가장 적절한 것은? 1-160323

Give children options and allow them to make their own decisions — on how much they would like to eat, whether they want to eat or not, and what they would like to have. For example, include them in the decision-making process of what you are thinking of making for dinner — "Lisa, would you like to have pasta and meatballs, or chicken and a baked potato?" When discussing how much they should eat during dinner, serve them a reasonable amount; if they claim they are still "hungry" after they are through, ask them to wait five to ten minutes, and if they continue to feel hunger, then they can have a second plate of food. These are fantastic behaviors that, when taught properly, teach brilliant self-confidence and self-control.

① Be a Role Model to Your Children
② Hunger: The Best Sauce for Children
③ Table Manners: Are They Important?
④ Good Nutrition: Children's Brain Power
⑤ Teach Children Food Independence

10 다음 글의 제목으로 가장 적절한 것은? 자체 제작 지문

Have you ever experienced this? You've probably experienced a lot of situations where you planned to do something, but you postponed your plans because you were busy or lazy, and you kept getting them delayed. But don't worry. Originally, most people put them off, which is a perfectly normal and natural phenomenon. If so, "Postpending" can be minimized as follows: You probably wrote all the plans for seven days of the week when you were writing them. And you would feel proud that I had written down enough plans. But remember, Sunday, *Magic Day*, is to leave the plans blank. Why is Sunday magical? As you know, it is very hard for you to keep all of your seven-day plans in full. So, when you set it blank when they are pushed back, the amount you can carry out your plans on Sunday will be more efficient and productive. So make sure to remember *Magic Day*.

① Empty your Day: To Live a More Indifferent Life Every Day
② The Way to Minimize Delaying Problem: Utilize Magic Day
③ Use Sunday to Maxmize The Profits of Industrial Society
④ Sunday: Procrastinators Appear The Most
⑤ Why Do You Postpone Your Plans?

11 다음 글의 제목으로 가장 적절한 것은?   1-170322

Studies from cities all over the world show the importance of life and activity as an urban attraction. People gather where things are happening and seek the presence of other people. Faced with the choice of walking down an empty or a lively street, most people would choose the street with life and activity. The walk will be more interesting and feel safer. Events where we can watch people perform or play music attract many people to stay and watch. Studies of benches and chairs in city space show that the seats with the best view of city life are used far more frequently than those that do not offer a view of other people.

① The City's Greatest Attraction: People
② Leave the City, Live in the Country
③ Make More Parks in the City
④ Feeling Lonely in the Crowded Streets
⑤ Ancient Cities Full of Tourist Attractions

12 다음 글의 제목으로 가장 적절한 것은?   1-170323

Consumers are generally uncomfortable with taking high risks. As a result, they are usually motivated to use a lot of strategies to reduce risk. Consumers can collect additional information by conducting online research, reading news articles, talking to friends or consulting an expert. Consumers also reduce uncertainty by buying the same brand that they did the last time, believing that the product should be at least as satisfactory as their last purchase. In addition, some consumers may employ a simple decision rule that results in a safer choice. For example, someone might buy the most expensive offering or choose a heavily advertised brand in the belief that this brand has higher quality than other brands.

① Lower Prices, Higher Sales
② Too Much Information Causes Stress
③ Advertisement: Noise for TV Viewers
④ Risktaking: A Source of Bigger Profits
⑤ Safe Purchase: What Consumers Pursue Eagerly

■ Day 7 Vocabulary

• discuss	논의하다, 토론하다	• attempt	시도하다, 시도
• virtuous	덕 있는, 고결한	• enrich	부유하게 하다, 풍성하게 하다, 비옥하게 하다
• brave	용감한	• face	직면하다, 마주하다
• reckless	무모한, 앞뒤를 가리지 않는	• fear	공포, 두려움
• consider	고려하다	• newborn	갓 태어난, 신생의
• gullible	잘 속는, 속이기 쉬운	• nutritious	영양가 있는, 영양이 풍부한
• trait	특성, 특징	• usual	보통의, 평소의, 흔히 하는
• deficiency	부족, 결핍	• starve	굶어 죽다
• maximize	극대화하다	• employee	직원
• well-being	안녕, 행복	• effecitve	효과적인
• suggestion	제안, 암시	• remain	남다, 여전히 ...이다
• virtue	덕목	• shed	오두막, 격납고
• midpoint	중점, 중심점	• corporate	단체의, 협력의, 법인(조직)의
• stingy	인색한, 너무 아끼는	• competent	유능한, 능력이 있는
• honesty	정직함	• relatively	상대적으로
• fundamental	근본적인	• developmental	개발적인
• advantage	이점	• initial	처음의, 초기의, 시초의
• approach	접근, 접근하다	• impression	인상
• escape	탈출, 탈출하다	• seek	찾다
• uncomfortable	불편한, 편하지 않은	• bother	방해하다
• reputation	명성, 평판	• professional	전문직의, 전문의, 직업의
• threaten	위협하다, 협박하다	• require	요구하다
• headache	두통	• humid	습기 있는
• poison	독	• achieve	달성하다, 이루다
• term	용어, 기간	• pitch	음, 던지다
• intention	의도	• linguist	언어학자
• comfort	위안하다, 위로하다, 편하게 하다	• tonal	음의, 색조의, 음색의
• businessman	사업가	• syllable	음절, 말 한 마디
• continually	계속해서	• specify	구체화하다
• government	정부	• survey	설문조사, 설문조사하다
• replace	대체하다	• occur	발생하다, 야기시키다
• courageous	용기 있는, 용감한	• frequently	빈번하게, 자주
• suppose	가정하다, 상상하다	• overall	전반적으로
• recommend	추천하다	• flourish	번창하다, 번성하다
• cliff	절벽, 낭떠러지	• region	지역, 부분, 범위, 분야

- conclusion   결론
- linguistic   언어학의, 언어학적인
- structure   구조, 구조물
- environment   환경
- advertisement   광고
- cite   인용, 인용하다
- statistical   통계상의
- cautious   신중한, 조심성 있는
- usually   대개, 보통의
- toothpaste   치약
- manufacture   제조하다
- dentist   치과 의사
- turn out   나타나다
- display   진열하다, 전시하다
- cosmetic   화장용의, 미용의
- rapidly   빨리, 급속히, 신속히
- wrinkle   주름
- evidence   증거
- objective   객관적인
- furthermore   게다가, 더욱이
- unfortunately   불행하게도
- typical   전형적인, 대표적인
- consumer   손님, 소비자
- judgement   판단
- claim   요구, 청구, 주장, 주장하다, 청구하다, 요구하다

01 1-190621

For almost all things in life, there can be too much of a good thing. Even the best things in life aren't so great in excess. This concept has been discussed at least as far back as Aristotle. He argued that being virtuous means finding a balance. For example, people should be brave, but if someone is too brave they become reckless. People should be trusting, but if someone is too trusting they are considered gullible For each of these traits, it is best to avoid both deficiency and excess. The best way is to live at the "sweet spot" that maximizes well-being. Aristotle's suggestion is that virtue is the midpoint, where someone is neither too generous nor too stingy, neither too afraid nor recklessly brave.

* excess: 과잉 **deliver: 잘 속아 넘어가는

① at the time of a biased decision

② in the area of material richness

③ away from social pressure

④ in the middle of two extremes

⑤ at the moment of instant pleasure

02 1-180330

Honesty is a fundamental part of every strong relationship. Use it to your advantage by being open with what you feel and giving a ① <u>truthful</u> opinion when asked. This approach can help you escape uncomfortable social situations and make friends with honest people. Follow this simple policy in life — never lie. When you ② <u>develop</u> a reputation for always telling the truth, you will enjoy strong relationships based on trust. It will also be more difficult to manipulate you. People who lie get into trouble when someone threatens to ③ <u>uncover</u> their lie. By living true to yourself, you'll ④ <u>avoid</u> a lot of headaches. Your relationships will also be free from the poison of lies and secrets. Don't be afraid to be honest with your friends, no matter how painful the truth is. In the long term, lies with good intentions ⑤ <u>comfort</u> people much more than telling the truth.

* manipulate: (사람을) 조종하다

03 1-150331

Armand Hammer was a great businessman who died in 1990 at the age of ninety-two. He was once asked how a man of his age had the energy to continually travel the world to do business and meet with heads of governments. He said, "I love my work. I can't wait to start a new day. I never wake up without being full of ideas. Everything is a challenge." George Bernard Shaw, one of the most successful writers of all time, said something similar about a hundred years earlier. He wrote, "I want to be thoroughly used up when I die, for the harder I work, the more I live." I think Hammer and Shaw would have agreed with me that nothing can replace _____ in life.

* throughly: 완전히, 철저히

① hard work
② true freindship
③ good education
④ witty comments
⑤ careful planning

04 1-150332

Let me give you a piece of advice that might change your mind about _____. Suppose that your doctor said that you have six months to live and recommended that you do everything you ever wanted to do. What would you do? Have you always wanted to sky dive, or climb cliffs, or maybe live alone in the woods for a month but been afraid you might be harmed? What difference would it make if you now attempted it? You'd almost certainly live through it and it would enrich the time you had left. Wouldn't it be nice to go out saying you had faced all your fears? Why do you wait till you have a death sentence? If it's that important to you, do it now.

* death sentence: 사형 선고

① being courageous
② helping others
③ making friends
④ recovering health
⑤ encouraging patients

05 1-150333

It is not always easy to eat well when you have a newborn baby. It can seem like you do not have time to prepare tasty nutritious meals or even to eat them. You will need to learn the following trick. Try not to wait until _____. When you have a newborn baby, preparing food will probably take longer than usual. If you start when you are already hungry, you will be absolutely starving before the food is ready. When you are starving and tired, eating healthy is difficult. You may want to eat fatty fast food, chocolates, cookies or chips. This type of food is okay sometimes, but not every day.

① your baby cries to be fed at night
② you find a new recipe for your meal
③ you are really hungry to think about eating
④ your kids finish all the food on thier plates
⑤ you feel like taking a nap after a heavy meal

06 1-160933

Millions of dollars and thousands of hours are spent each year trying to teach managers how to coach their employees and give them effective feedback. Yet much of this training is ineffective, and many managers remain poor coaches. Is that because this can't be trained? No, that's not the reason. Research sheds light on why corporate training often fails. Studies by Peter Hesling and his colleagues show that many managers _____. These managers judge employees as competent or incompetent at the start and that's that. They do relatively little developmental coaching and when employees do improve, they may fail to take notice, remaining stuck in their initial impression. What's more, they are far less likely to seek or accept critical feedback from their employees. Why bother to coach employees if they can't change and why get feedback from them if you can't change?

① provide few financial incentives
② change their decisions too often
③ do not believe in personal change
④ set their goals unrealistically high
⑤ take risks without careful consideration

07 1-160934

Opera singers and dry air don't get along. In fact, the best professional singers require humid settings to help them achieve the right pitch. If the amount of moisture in the air influences musical pitch, linguist Caleb Everett wondered, has that translated into the development of fewer tonal languages in locations lacking moisture? In tonal languages, such as Mandarin Chinese, the same syllable spoken at a higher pitch can specify a different word if spoken at a lower pitch. In a survey of more than 3,700 languages, he found that those with complex tones do occur less frequently in dry areas than in humid ones. Overall, only one in 30 complex tonal languages flourished in dry areas; one in three non-tonal languages appeared in those same regions. Those conclusions go against a linguistic view that the structure of language _____.

① can be acquired through repetition
② is independent of its environment
③ can change gradually over time
④ affects how we see the world
⑤ is influenced by musical pitch

08 1-190641

Many advertisements cite statistical surveys. But we should be (a) <u>cautious</u> because we usually do not know how these surveys are conducted. For example, a toothpaste manufacturer once had a poster that said, "More than 80% of dentists recommend Smiley Toothpaste." This seems to say that most dentists (b) <u>prefer</u> Smiley Toothpaste to other brands. But it turns out that the survey questions allowed the dentists to recommend more than one brand, and in fact another competitor's brand was recommended just as often as Smiley Toothpaste! No wonder the UK Advertising Standards Authority ruled in 2007 that the poster was (c) <u>misleading</u> and it could no longer be displayed. A similar case concerns a well-known cosmetics firm marketing a cream that is supposed to rapidly reduce wrinkles. But the only evidence provided is that "76% of 50 women agreed." But what this means is that the evidence is based on just the personal opinions from a small sample with no objective measurement of their skin's condition. Furthermore, we are not told how these women were selected. Without such information, the "evidence" provided is pretty much (d) <u>useful</u>. Unfortunately, such advertisements are quite typical, and as consumers we just have to use our own judgement and (e) <u>avoid</u> taking advertising claims too seriously.

① The Link between Advertisements and the Economy
② Are Statistical Data in Advertisements Reliable?
③ Statistics in Advertisements Are Objective!
④ The Bright Side of Public Advertisements
⑤ Quality or Price, Which Matters More?

Assignment of Day 7

01 밑줄 친 <u>Going abroad</u>가 다음 글에서 의미하는 바로 가장 적절한 것은?

모의고사 변형 문제

Sometimes, you feel the need to avoid something that will lead to success out of discomfort. Maybe you are avoiding extra work because you are tired. You are actively shutting out success because you want to avoid being uncomfortable. Therefore, overcoming your instinct to avoid uncomfortable things at first is essential. Try doing new things outside of your comfort zone. Change is always uncomfortable, but it is key to doing things differently in order to find that magical formula for success. In other words, <u>Going abroad</u> may be a good option rather than going to the area you originally know.

① Challenging familiar things by setting step-by-step goals
② Improving your ability to try things you haven't experienced to overcome your anxiety
③ Attempting to untried things to succeed even though you are in discomfort
④ Visiting other countries to stack enough global experiences
⑤ Making new passport to go other countries

02 밑줄 친 "<u>There is no there there</u>"가 다음 글에서 의미하는 바로 가장 적절한 것은?

1-190921

I believe the second decade of this new century is already very different. There are, of course, still millions of people who equate success with money and power — who are determined to never get off that treadmill despite the cost in terms of their well-being, relationships, and happiness. There are still millions desperately looking for the next promotion, the next million-dollar payday that they believe will satisfy their longing to feel better about themselves, or silence their dissatisfaction. But both in the West and in emerging economies, there are more people every day who recognize that these are all dead ends — that they are chasing a broken dream. That we cannot find the answer in our current definition of success alone because—as Gertrude Stein once said of Oakland — "<u>There is no there there.</u>"

① People are losing confidence in themselves.
② Without dreams, there is no chance for growth.
③ We should not live according to others' expectations.
④ It is hard to realize our potential in difficult situations.
⑤ Money and power do not necessarily lead you to success.

03 밑줄 친 "<u>learn and live.</u>"가 다음 글에서 의미하는 바로 가장 적절한 것은?

1-191121

There is a critical factor that determines whether your choice will influence that of others: the visible consequences of the choice. Take the case of the Adélie penguins. They are often found strolling in large groups toward the edge of the water in search of food. Yet danger awaits in the icy-cold water. There is the leopard seal, for one, which likes to have penguins for a meal. What is an Adélie to do? The penguins' solution is to play the waiting game. They wait and wait and wait by the edge of the water until one of them gives up and jumps in. The moment that occurs, the rest of the penguins watch with anticipation to see what happens next. If the pioneer survives, everyone else will follow suit. If it perishes, they'll turn away. One penguin's destiny alters the fate of all the others. Their strategy, you could say, is "<u>learn and live.</u>"

* perish: 죽다

① occupy a rival's territory for safety
② discover who the enemy is and attack first
③ share survival skills with the next generation
④ support the leader's decisions for the best results
⑤ follow another's action only when it is proven safe

04 (A), (B), (C)의 각 네모 안에서 문맥에 맞는 낱말로 가장 적절한 것은?

1-211130

For species approaching extinction, zoos can act as a last chance for survival. ① <u>Recovery</u> programs are established to coordinate the efforts of field conservationists and wildlife authorities. As populations of those species ② <u>diminish</u> it is not unusual for zoos to start captive breeding programs. Captive breeding acts to protect against extinction. In some cases captive-bred individuals may be released back into the wild, supplementing wild populations. This is most successful in situations where individuals are at greatest threat during a ③ <u>particular</u> life stage. For example, turtle eggs may be removed from high-risk locations until after they hatch. This may ④ <u>increase</u> the number of turtles that survive to adulthood. Crocodile programs have also been successful in protecting eggs and hatchlings, ⑤ <u>capturing</u> hatchlings once they are better equipped to protect themselves.

* captive-breeding: 포획 사육 **hatch: 부화하다

In small towns the same workman makes chairs and doors and tables, and often the same person builds houses. And it is, of course, impossible for a man of many trades to be skilled in all of them. In large cities, on the other hand, because many people make demands on each trade, one trade alone — very often even less than a whole trade — is enough to support a man. For instance, one man makes shoes for men, and another for women. And there are places even where one man earns a living by only stitching shoes, another by cutting them out, and another by sewing the uppers together. Such skilled workers may have used simple tools, but their _____ did result in more efficient and productive work.

① specialization
② criticism
③ competition
④ diligence
⑤ imagination

About four billion years ago, molecules joined together to form cells. About two billion years later, cells joined together to form more complex cells. And then a billion years later, these more complex cells joined together to form multicellular organisms. All of these evolved because the participating individuals could, by working together, spread their genetic material in new and more effective ways. Fastforward another billion years to our world, which is full of social animals, from ants to wolves to humans. The same principle applies. Ants and wolves in groups can do things that no single ant or wolf can do, and we humans, by _____, have become the earth's dominant species.

① cooperating with one another
② fighting against enemies
③ studying other species
④ inventing various machines
⑤ paying attention to differences

07 다음 빈칸에 들어갈 말로 가장 적절한 것은? 1-170333

What do advertising and map-making have in common? Without doubt the best answer is their shared need to communicate a limited version of the truth. An advertisement must create an image that's appealing and a map must present an image that's clear, but neither can meet its goal by _____.
Ads will cover up or play down negative aspects of the company or service they advertise. In this way, they can promote a favorable comparison with similar products or differentiate a product from its competitors. Likewise, the map must remove details that would be confusing.

① reducing the amount of information
② telling or showing everything
③ listening to people's voices
④ relying on visual images only
⑤ making itself available to everyone

08 다음 빈칸에 들어갈 말로 가장 적절한 것은? 1-170334

Did you know you actually think in images and not in words? Images are simply mental pictures showing ideas and experiences. Early humans communicated their ideas and experiences to others for thousands of years by drawing pictures in the sand or on the walls of their caves. Only recently have humans created various languages and alphabets to symbolize these "picture" messages. Your mind has not yet adapted to this relatively new development. An image has a much greater impact on your brain than words; the nerves from the eye to the brain are twenty-five times larger than the nerves from the ear to the brain. You often remember a person's face but not his or her name, for example. The old saying, "_____," is true.

① Actions speak louder than words
② A bad workman blames his tools
③ You can't judge a book by its cover
④ The pen is mightier than the sword
⑤ A picture is worth a thousand words

09 다음 빈칸에 들어갈 말로 가장 적절한 것은?   1-180631

One outcome of motivation is behavior that takes considerable _____. For example, if you are motivated to buy a good car, you will research vehicles online, look at ads, visit dealerships, and so on. Likewise, if you are motivated to lose weight, you will buy lowfat foods, eat smaller portions, and exercise. Motivation not only drives the final behaviors that bring a goal closer but also creates willingness to expend time and energy on preparatory behaviors. Thus, someone motivated to buy a new smartphone may earn extra money for it, drive through a storm to reach the store, and then wait in line to buy it.

* preparatory: 준비의

① risk   ② effort   ③ memory
④ fortune   ⑤ experience

10 다음 빈칸에 들어갈 말로 가장 적절한 것은?   1-180632

Good managers have learned to overcome the initial feelings of anxiety when assigning tasks. They are aware that no two people act in exactly the same way and so do not feel threatened if they see one employee going about a task differently than another. Instead, they focus on _____. If a job was successfully done, as long as people are working in a manner acceptable to the organization (for example, as long as salespeople are keeping to the company's ethical selling policy), then that's fine. If an acceptable final outcome wasn't achieved, then such managers respond by discussing it with the employee and analyzing the situation, to find out what training or additional skills that person will need to do the task successfully in the future.

* assign: (일·책임 등을) 맡기다

① the end result
② the welfare policy
③ the uniform procedure
④ the informal atmosphere
⑤ the employee's personality

11 다음 빈칸에 들어갈 말로 가장 적절한 것은?   1-180633

There is good evidence that in organic development, perception starts with _____. For example, when two-year-old children and chimpanzees had learned that, of two boxes presented to them, the one with a triangle of a particular size and shape always contained attractive food, they had no difficulty applying their training to triangles of very different appearance. The triangles were made smaller or larger or turned upside down. A black triangle on a white background was replaced by a white triangle on a black background, or an outlined triangle by a solid one. These changes seemed not to interfere with recognition. Similar results were obtained with rats. Karl Lashley, a psychologist, has asserted that simple transpositions of this type are universal in all animals including humans.

* transposition: 치환

① interpreting different gestures
② establishing social frameworks
③ identifying the information of colors
④ separating the self from the environment
⑤ recognizing outstanding structural features

12 다음 빈칸에 들어갈 말로 가장 적절한 것은?   자체 제작 지문

Demand is the consumer's desire to purchase a product, and supply is the supplier's desire to sell the product. The supply and demand law shows this relationship between supply and demand. demand decreases because when the price of a product increases, consumers will not want to buy it. However, supply increases because when the price of a product increases, suppliers want to sell it at a higher price. Therefore, demand decreases as prices increase, but this is not the only reason that demand decreases. Substitute goods refer to products that can be used as an alternative to a certain product. If you like coke, but the price of another alternative called soda decreases, you will want to buy that alternative. The demand for coke decreased because it is sufficient to satisfy your needs, so _____.

① you drink coke because of its lower prices
② you will choose a lower-priced soda, an alternative
③ supply for coke will decrease because of the supply and demand law
④ soda is perfect alternative because of its high prices
⑤ you won't drink soda instead of coke

13 다음 글을 읽고, 두 물음에 답하시오.

A quick look at history shows that humans have not always had the abundance of food that is enjoyed throughout most of the developed world today. In fact, there have been numerous times in history when food has been rather scarce. As a result, people used to eat more when food was available since the availability of the next meal was (a) questionable. Over-eating in those times was essential to ensure survival, and humans received satisfaction from eating more than was needed for immediate purposes. On top of that, the highest pleasure was derived from eating the most calorie-dense foods, resulting in a (b) longer lasting energy reserve. Even though there are parts of the world where, unfortunately, food is still scarce, most of the world's population today has plenty of food available to survive and thrive. However, this abundance is new, and your body has not caught up, still naturally (c) rewarding you for eating more than you need and for eating the most calorie-dense foods. These are innate habits and not simple addictions. They are self-preserving mechanisms initiated by your body, ensuring your future survival, but they are (d) irrelevant now. Therefore, it is your responsibility to communicate with your body regarding the new environment of food abundance and the need to (e) strengthen the inborn habit of over-eating.

윗 글의 제목으로 가장 적절한것은?

① Which Is Better, Tasty or Health Food?
② Simple Steps for a More Balanced Diet
③ Over-eating: It's Rooted in Our Genes
④ How Calorie-dense Foods Ruin Our Bodies
⑤ Our Eating Habits Reflect Our Personalities

밑줄 친 (a)~(e) 중에서 문맥상 낱말의 쓰임이 적절하지 않은 것은?

① (a) ② (b) ③ (c) ④ (d) ⑤ (e)

Day 8 Vocabulary

• audience	청중, 관객
• centered	중심이 있는, 중심이 있는
• monitor	감시하다, 모니터링하다
• indicate	나타내다
• assist	돕다
• issue	쟁점, 논란
• session	세션, 기간, 회의
• memorize	암기하다, 기억하다
• script	대본, 스크립트
• on-stage anxiety	무대공포증
• respectful	존경하는
• multiple	다수의, 배수의, 곱하다
• encourage	독려하다, 장려하다
• engage	약속하다, 관여시키다
• emotionally	감정적으로
• tend to	–하려는 경향이 있다
• repeated	반복된, 반복되는
• appreciate	진가를 알아보다, 인정하다, 감사하다
• leisure	자유 시간, 틈, 여가
• touch	만지다, 접촉, 감동적인
• depsite	–에도 불구하고
• familiarity	친근감, 유대감
• renewed	새롭게 한, 다시 시작한
• destination	목적지, 행선지
• immense	거대한, 막대한, 헤아릴 수 없는
• benefit	혜택, 이점
• hesitate	주저하다, 망설이다
• childhood	어릴 적, 어린 시절
• (a) lot(s) of firsts	처음 보는 것이 많은
• go through	통과하다, 지나가다
• pain	고통
• in common	공통적으로
• rap	톡톡 두드림, 질책, 평판
• recent	최근의
• physical contact	물리적 접촉, 육체적 접촉

• briefly	간략하게, 짧게
• participant	참여자
• illustrate	설명하다, 삽화를 넣다
• mere	단지, 단순한, 단지 –에 불과한
• interpersonal	인간 사이의 존재하는, 대인 관계의
• temporarily	일시적으로, 일시로
• unintentional	의도하지 않은, 고의가 아닌
• thereafter	그 후에, 그 이래
• behavior	행동
• promote	촉진시키다, 홍보하다, 승진하다
• participate	참여하다, 참가하다
• individually	개별적으로, 낱개로
• place	장소, 곳, 군데
• retrieve	되찾다
• ape	유인원, 꼬리 없는 원숭이
• distinguish	구별하다
• predict	예측하다
• feature	특징, 특색, 특징으로 삼다
• attractive	매력적인, 사람의 마음을 이끄는
• problematic	문제의, 문제가 있는
• guarantee	보증하다
• relation	관계, 관련
• assurance	보증, 보장
• unlike	–와 달리
• consistency	일관성, 언행일치
• strategy	전략, 전술
• solely	다만, 단지, 혼자서
• extension	확장, 팽창, 연장
• facility	시설
• merchandise	정비공, 기계공
• souvenirs	기념품
• beverage	음료
• essential	필수적인, 본질적인
• reliable	신뢰할 수 있는
• core product	핵심 제품

문장 맥락, 순서, 삽입, 요약문

01 1-190335

Public speaking is audience centered because speakers "listen" to their audiences during speeches. They monitor audience feedback, the verbal and non-verbal signals an audience gives a speaker. ① Audience feedback often indicates whether listeners understand, have interest in, and are ready to accept the speaker's ideas. ② This feedback assists the speaker in many ways. ③ It helps the speaker know when to slow down, explain something more carefully, or even tell the audience that she or he will return to an issue in a question-and-answer session at the close of the speech. ④ It is important for the speaker to memorize his or her script to reduce on-stage anxiety. ⑤ Audience feedback assists the speaker in creating a respectful connection with the audience.

*verbal: 언어적인

02 1-160635

The habit of reading books multiple times encourages people to engage with them emotionally. If they only read a book once, they tend to only focus on the events and stories in it.

(A) The same effect can be seen with familiar holiday destinations. Revisiting a place can also help people better understand both the place and themselves. Considering the immense benefits, don't hesitate to give re-consuming a try.

(B) By enjoying the emotional effects of the book more deeply, people become more in touch with their own feelings. Despite their familarity with the stories, rereading brings renewed understanding of both the book and themselves.

(C) But with a second read-through, the repeated experience brings back the initial emotions caused by the book, and allows people to appreciate those emotions at their leisure.

① (A) – (C) – (B)

② (B) – (A) – (C)

③ (B) – (C) – (A)

④ (C) – (A) – (B)

⑤ (C) – (B) – (A)

When you hit puberty, however, sometimes these forever-friendships go through growing pains.

Childhood friends — friends you've known forever — are really special. (①) They know everything about you, and you've shared lots of firsts. (②) You find that you have less in common than you used to. (③) Maybe you're into rap and she's into pop, or you go to different schools and have different groups of friends. (④) Change can be scary, but remember: Friends, even best friends, don't have to be exactly alike. (⑤) Having friends with other interests keeps life interesting — just think of what you can learn from each other.

* puberty: 사춘기

04 1-180640

Recent studies point to the importance of warm physical contact for healthy relationships with others. In one study, participants who briefly held a cup of hot (versus iced) coffee judged a target person as having a "warmer" personality (generous, caring); in another study, participants holding a hot (versus cold) pack were more likely to choose a gift for a friend instead of something for themselves. These findings illustrate that mere contact experiences of physical warmth activate feelings of interpersonal warmth. Moreover, this temporarily increased activation of interpersonal warmth feelings then influences judgments toward other people in an unintentional manner. Such feelings activated in one context last for a while thereafter and have influence on judgment and behavior in later contexts without the person's awareness.

Experiencing physical warmth ___(A)___ interpersonal warmth, which happens in an ___(B)___ way

---

	(A)	(B)
①	promotes	flexible
②	promotes	automatic
③	affects	inconsistent
④	minimizes	obvious
⑤	minimizes	rapid

05 1-180940

At the Leipzig Zoo in Germany, 34 zoo chimpanzees and orangutans participating in a study were each individually tested in a room, where they were put in front of two boxes. An experimenter would place an object inside one box and leave the room. Another experimenter would enter the room, move the object into the other box and exit. When the first experimenter returned and tried retrieving the object from the first box, the great ape would help the experimenter open the second box, which it knew the object had been transferred to. However, most apes in the study did not help the first experimenter open the second box if the first experimenter was still in the room to see the second experimenter move the item. The findings show the great apes understood when the first experimenter still thought the item was where he or she last left it.

According to the study, great apes can distinguish whether or not people have a ___(A)___ belief about reality and use this understanding to ___(B)___ people.

	(A)	(B)
①	false	help
②	ehtical	obey
③	scientific	imitate
④	irrational	deceive
⑤	widespread	correct

06 1-181140

We cannot predict the outcomes of sporting contests, which vary from week to week. This heterogeneity is a feature of sport. It is the uncertainty of the result and the quality of the contest that consumers find attractive. For the sport marketer, this is problematic, as the quality of the contest cannot be guaranteed, no promises can be made in relations to the result and no assurances can be given in respect of the performance of star players. Unlike consumer products, sport cannot and does not display consistency as a key feature of marketing strategies. The sport marketer therefore must avoid marketing strategies based solely on winning, and must instead focus on developing product extensions such as the facility, parking, merchandise, souvenirs, food and beverages rather than on the core product (that is, the game itself).

* heretogeneity: 이질성(異質性)

Sport has the essential nature of being _____(A)_____, which requires that its marketing strategies _____(B)_____ products and services more than just the sports match.

	(A)	(B)
①	unreliable	feature
②	unreliable	exclude
③	risky	ignore
④	consistent	involve
⑤	consistent	promote

01 다음 글에서 전체 흐름과 관계 <u>없는</u> 문장은? 1-160339

The water that is embedded in our food and manufactured products is called "virtual water." For example, about 265 gallons of water is needed to produce two pounds of wheat. ① So, the virtual water of these two pounds of wheat is 265 gallons. ② Virtual water is also present in dairy products, soups, beverages, and liquid medicines. ③ However, it is necessary to drink as much water as possible to stay healthy. ④ Every day, humans consume lots of virtual water and the content of virtual water varies according to products. ⑤ For instance, to produce two pounds of meat requires about 5 to 10 times as much water as to produce two pounds of vegetables.

* virtual water: 공산품 · 농축산물의 제조 · 재배에 드는 물

02 다음 글에서 전체 흐름과 관계 <u>없는</u> 문장은? 1-161139

Asians and many Native American cultures view silence as an important and appropriate part of social interaction. ① Speakers from these cultures often use some moments of silence before offering a response to another speaker. ② Silence causes division and separation, creating serious problems in relationships. ③ Such initial silence conveys the listener's respect for the speaker; it indicates that the listener has heard the speaker's words and is giving them due thought. ④ Silence is viewed as a time to learn, to think about, and to review what the speaker has said. ⑤ In cultures that prize silence, responding too quickly after speakers have finished their turns is interpreted as having devoted inadequate attention and consideration to speakers' words and thoughts.

03 주어진 글 다음에 이어질 글의 순서로 가장 적절한 것을 고르시오. 1-170935

> Use a plastic pen and rub it on your hair about ten times and then hold the pen close to small pieces of tissue paper or chalk dust.

(A) During a thunderstorm, clouds may become charged as they rub against each other. The lightning that we often see during a storm is caused by a large flow of electrical charges between charged clouds and the earth.

(B) This kind of electricity is produced by friction, and the pen becomes electrically charged. Static electricity is also found in the atmosphere.

(C) You will find that the bits of paper or chalk dust cling to the pen. What you have done there is to create a form of electricity called static electricity.

① (A) - (C) - (B)　　② (B) - (A) - (C)
③ (B) - (C) - (A)　　④ (C) - (A) - (B)
⑤ (C) - (B) - (A)

04 주어진 글 다음에 이어질 글의 순서로 가장 적절한 것을 고르시오. 1-170936

> From a correlational observation, we conclude that one variable is related to a second variable. But neither behavior could be directly causing the other even though there is a relationship.

(A) They found the best predictor to be the number of tattoos the rider had. It would be a ridiculous error to conclude that tattoos cause motorcycle accidents or that motorcycle accidents cause tattoos.

(B) The following example will illustrate why it is difficult to make causal statements on the basis of correlational observation. The researchers at the U.S. Army conducted a study of motorcycle accidents, attempting to correlate the number of accidents with other variables such as socio-economic level and age.

(C) Obviously, a third variable is related to both — perhaps preference for risk. A person who is willing to take risks likes to be tattooed and also takes more chances on a motorcycle.

* variable: 변인

① (A) - (C) - (B)　　② (B) - (A) - (C)
③ (B) - (C) - (A)　　④ (C) - (A) - (B)
⑤ (C) - (B) - (A)

When the boy learned that he had misspelled the word, he went to the judges and told them.

Some years ago at the national spelling bee in Washington, D.C., a thirteen-year-old boy was asked to spell echolalia, a word that means a tendency to repeat whatever one hears. (①) Although he misspelled the word, the judges misheard him, told him he had spelled the word right, and allowed him to advance. (②) So he was eliminated from the competition after all. (③) Newspaper headlines the next day called the honest young man a "spelling bee hero," and his photo appeared in The New York Times. (④) "The judges said I had a lot of honesty," the boy told reporters. (⑤) He added that part of his motive was, "I didn't want to feel like a liar."

* spelling bee: 단어 철자 맞히기 대회

Instead of that, say to them, 'I can't deal with that now but what I can do is I can ask Brian to give you a hand and he should be able to explain them.'

Whenever you say what you can't do, say what you can do. This ends a sentence on a positive note and has a much lower tendency to cause someone to challenge it. (①) Consider this situation — a colleague comes up to you and asks you to look over some figures with them before a meeting they are having tomorrow. (②) You simply say, 'No, I can't deal with this now.' (③) This may then lead to them insisting how important your input is, increasing the pressure on you to give in. (④) Or, 'I can't deal with that now but I can find you in about half an hour when I have finished.' (⑤) Either of these types of responses are better than ending it with a negative.

07 다음 글의 내용을 한 문장으로 요약하고자 한다. 빈칸 (A), (B)에 들어갈 말로 가장 적절한 것은? 1-170340

A large American hardware manufacturer was invited to introduce its products to a distributor with good reputation in Germany. Wanting to make the best possible impression, the American company sent its most promising young executive, Fred Wagner, who spoke fluent German. When Fred first met his German hosts, he shook hands firmly, greeted everyone in German, and even remembered to bow the head slightly as is the German custom. Fred, a very effective public speaker, began his presentation with a few humorous jokes to set a relaxed atmosphere. However, he felt that his presentation was not very well received by the German executives. Even though Fred thought he had done his cultural homework, he made one particular error. Fred did not win any points by telling a few jokes. It was viewed as too informal and unprofessional in a German business setting.

* distributor: 배급 업체

This story shows that using (A) in a business setting can be considered (B) in Germany.

	(A)	(B)
①	humor	essential
②	humor	inappropriate
③	gestures	essential
④	gestures	inappropriate
⑤	first names	useful

08 다음 글의 내용을 한 문장으로 요약하고자 한다. 빈칸 (A), (B)에 들어갈 말로 가장 적절한 것은? 1-170640

According to an Australian study, a person's confidence in the kitchen is linked to the kind of food that he or she tends to enjoy eating. Compared to the average person, those who are proud of the dishes they make are more likely to enjoy eating vegetarian food and health food. Moreover, this group is more likely than the average person to enjoy eating diverse kinds of food: from salads and seafood to hamburgers and hot chips. In contrast, people who say "I would rather clean than make dishes." don't share this wide-ranging enthusiasm for food. They are less likely than the average person to enjoy different types of food. In general, they eat out less than the average person except for when it comes to eating at fast food restaurants

In general, people who are confident in (A) are more likely to enjoy (B) foods than those who are not.

	(A)	(B)
①	cooking	various
②	cooking	specific
③	tasting	organic
④	dieting	healthy
⑤	dieting	exotic

09 다음 글의 내용을 한 문장으로 요약하고자 한다. 빈칸 (A), (B)에 들어갈 말로 가장 적절한 것은? 1-170940

Social psychologists at the University of Virginia asked college students to stand at the base of a hill while carrying a weighted backpack and estimate the steepness of the hill. Some participants stood next to close friends whom they had known a long time, some stood next to friends they had not known for long, some stood next to strangers, and the others stood alone during the exercise. The participants who stood with close friends gave significantly lower estimates of the steepness of the hill than those who stood alone, next to strangers, or next to newly formed friends. Furthermore, the longer the close friends had known each other, the less steep the hill appeared to the participants involved in the study.

According to the study, a task is perceived as less (A) when standing next to a (B) friend.

	(A)	(B)
①	difficult	close
②	valuable	new
③	difficult	smart
④	valuable	patient
⑤	exciting	strong

10 다음 글의 내용을 한 문장으로 요약하고자 한다. 빈칸 (A), (B)에 들어갈 말로 가장 적절한 것은? 1-171140

If you want to modify people's behavior, is it better to highlight the benefits of changing or the costs of not changing? According to Peter Salovey, one of the originators of the concept of emotional intelligence, it depends on whether they perceive the new behavior as safe or risky. If they think the behavior is safe, we should emphasize all the good things that will happen if they do it — they'll want to act immediately to obtain those certain gains. But when people believe a behavior is risky, that approach doesn't work. They're already comfortable with the status quo, so the benefits of change aren't attractive, and the stop system kicks in. Instead, we need to destabilize the status quo and emphasize the bad things that will happen if they don't change. Taking a risk is more appealing when they're faced with a guaranteed loss if they don't. The prospect of a certain loss brings the go system online.

* status quo: 현재 상태

The way to modify people's behavior depends on their (A) : if the new behavior is regarded as safe, emphasizing the rewards works but if regarded as risky, highlighting the loss of staying (B) works.

	(A)	(B)
①	perception	changed
②	perception	unchanged
③	recognition	changed
④	consistency	unchanged
⑤	consistency	focused

Day 9 Vocabulary

- ethical   도덕적인, 윤리적인
- require   요구하다, 필요로 하다
- immediate   즉각적인, 즉시
- beyond   너머에
- personal   개인적, 개인의
- need   필요, 의무, 책임
- desire   갈망, 욕구, 갈망하다
- consequence   결과, 귀결, 중요성
- elemental   원소의, 기본적인
- sense   감각
- moral   도덕적인
- various   다양한
- interaction   상호작용
- sense   감각
- dramatic   극적인, 연극같은
- virtual   가상의, 실직적인
- rehearsal   리허설, 예행연습
- examine   조사하다, 검토하다
- course   진로, 방향, 진행, 전진
- determine   결심하다
- morally   도덕적으로, 정신적으로
- capacity   수용력, 용량
- empathy   동정, 공감
- have no idea   전혀 모르다
- affect   영향을 끼치다
- conceive   마음에 품다, 생각해내다

Day 9: 영어 모의고사 내신은 어떻게 풀어나가야 하는가 4(어법 및 서술형)

#모의고사 문법은 주로 어떤 문법이 출제되는가?

■ 1-131134

#아래 지문을 읽고, 지문에 대한 서술형으로 출제될만한 문제를 떠올려보자.

Ethical decision making requires us to look beyond the immediate moment and beyond personal needs and desires to imagine the possible consequences of our choices and behavior on self and others. In its most elemental sense, moral imagination is about picturing various outcomes in our interactions with others. In some sense, moral imagination is a dramatic virtual rehearsal that allows us to examine different courses of action to determine the morally best thing to do. The capacity for empathy is crucial to moral imagination. As we have no immediate experience of what others feel, we can have no idea of how they are affected. Only by conceiving what we ourselves would feel in the situation can we understand how they feel.

Assignment of Day 9

01 다음 글에서 밑줄 친 부분중 어법적으로 틀린 것은?   1-150328

One cool thing about my Uncle Arthur was ① <u>what</u> he could always pick the best places to camp. One time, we went to Garrison Rock. Uncle Arthur said that the Indians stayed there. On trips like this, he would always have a good story ② <u>to tell</u>. His stories were always aimed at ③ <u>helping</u> us children use our brains to get out of trouble. For example, one story was about a guy being ④ <u>chased</u> by a big dog. They ran into a field. We kids were thinking that the dog would catch him. But the guy saw a bathtub in the field. He ran to the bathtub and ⑤ <u>pulled</u> it over himself. The dog just barked and barked until it went away. Then the guy came out of the bathtub, and went home.

02 다음 글에서 밑줄 친 부분중 어법적으로 틀린 것은?   1-160328

Your parents may be afraid that you will not spend your allowance wisely. You may make some foolish spending choices, but if you ① <u>do</u>, the decision to do so is your own and hopefully you will learn from your mistakes. Much of learning ② <u>occurs</u> through trial and error. Explain to your parents that money is something you will have to deal with for the rest of your life. It is better ③ <u>what</u> you make your mistakes early on rather than later in life. Explain that you will have a family someday and you need to know how ④ <u>to manage</u> your money. Not everything ⑤ <u>is taught</u> at school!

Take time to read the comics. This is worthwhile not just because they will make you laugh but ① <u>because</u> they contain wisdom about the nature of life. Charlie Brown and Blondie are part of my morning routine and help me ② <u>to start</u> the day with a smile. When you read the comics section of the newspaper, ③ <u>cutting</u> out a cartoon that makes you laugh. Post it wherever you need it most, such as on your refrigerator or at work — so that every time you see it, you will smile and feel your spirit ④ <u>lifted.</u> Share your favorites with your friends and family so that everyone can get a good laugh, too. Take your comics with you when you go to visit sick friends ⑤ <u>who</u> can really use a good laugh.

My dad worked very late hours as a musician —until about three in the morning —so he slept late on weekends. As a result, we didn't have much of a relationship when I was young other than him constantly nagging me to take care of chores like mowing the lawn and cutting the hedges, ① <u>which</u> I hated. He was a responsible man ② <u>dealing</u> with an irresponsible kid. Memories of how we interacted ③ <u>seems</u> funny to me today. For example, one time he told me to cut the grass and I decided ④ <u>to do</u> just the front yard and postpone doing the back, but then it rained for a couple days and the backyard grass became so high I had to cut it with a sickle. That took so long ⑤ <u>that</u> by the time I was finished, the front yard was too high to mow, and so on.

* sickle: 낫

Bad lighting can increase stress on your eyes, as can light that is too bright, or light that shines ① <u>directly</u> into your eyes. Fluorescent lighting can also be ② <u>tiring</u>. What you may not appreciate is that the quality of light may also be important. Most people are happiest in bright sunshine — this may cause a release of chemicals in the body ③ <u>that</u> bring a feeling of emotional well-being. Artificial light, which typically contains only a few wavelengths of light, ④ <u>do</u> not seem to have the same effect on mood that sunlight has. Try experimenting with working by a window or ⑤ <u>using</u> full spectrum bulbs in your desk lamp. You will probably find that this improves the quality of your working environment.

* fluorescent lighting: 형광등

There are many methods for finding answers to the mysteries of the universe, and science is only one of these. However, science is unique. Instead of making guesses, scientists follow a system ① <u>designed</u> to prove if their ideas are true or false. They constantly re-examine and test their theories and conclusions. Old ideas are replaced when scientists find new information ② <u>that</u> they cannot explain. Once somebody makes a discovery, others review it carefully before ③ <u>using</u> the information in their own research. This way of building new knowledge on older discoveries ④ <u>ensure</u> that scientists correct their mistakes. Armed with scientific knowledge, people build tools and machines that transform the way we live, making our lives ⑤ <u>much</u> easier and better.

It is said that you never forget your first love. But you should, because memories of it can destroy your relationships for life. Sociologists found that the happiness of young love can become an unreal standard by which all future romances are judged. According to a report, [A] 장기간의 행복을 보장하는 최고의 방법 in a relationship is not to stick to your first love. People with a more practical view of relationships tend to have more successful longterm ones. Because they don't try to recreate the strong passion they once shared with a past lover.

아래 보기를 활용하여 [A]에 해당되는 문장을 영작하시오.

```
[보기]
- 총 8단어로 영작할 것.
- to부정사와 최상급을 사용할 것
- 필요시 형태나 시제를 변형하여 서술할 것.
- long-term/ make sure을 반드시 포함할 것.
```

_____

[A] meet/ people/ we/ all/ people/ their lives/ in the narrowest possible terms/ limit. They are determined to stay in a limited comfort zone. Some people avoid the opportunity to make a public presentation because it makes them nervous. Others reject a chance to study abroad because they don't consider themselves adventurous. People become trapped by their own conception of their limits, so they become angry at even being asked to step beyond them. This attitude toward life, however, is a huge mistake. Welcome new challenges at every turn, saying yes as often as possible.

아래 보기를 활용하여 [A]에 해당되는 문장을 서술하시오.

```
[보기]
- 총 14단어로 영작할 것.
- 현재완료 구문을 사용할 것.
- 주격 관계대명사를 사용할 것.
- 필요시 형태나 시제를 변형하여 서술할 것.
```

_____

09 다음 글을 읽고 아래 물음에 답하시오.   1-140319

It is very important to help poor countries, but it's not simple. We should be giving money or food directly to the poor in emergencies like an earthquake or flood. In less emergent situations, however, providing food can make people dependent. If a developed country gives food to a poor country, its local farmers will find it difficult to produce food to sell. We need to help poor people to earn their own money, or to produce their own food. Just giving them money or food is not a good idea. We have to find a way to help them stand on their own two feet.

밑줄 친 필자가 생각하는 주장의 근거를 본문에서 찾아 한국어로 서술하시오.

_____

_____

10 다음 글을 읽고 아래 물음에 답하시오.   1-150319

Some people need money more than we do. For example, some people have (a) lost their homes due to natural disasters or war, while others don't have enough food or clothing. So this year, for our birthdays, let's tell our friends and family to (b) donate money to a charity instead of buying us presents. I know that some kids might (c) not want to give up their birthday presents, and I understand. However, remember that we can live (d) with new toys or games more easily than someone can live without food, clothing, or shelter. So, we should tell our friends and family (e) that, for our birthdays this year, we want to give to others.

밑줄 친(a)~(e)에서 문맥적으로, 혹은 어법적으로 어색한 곳을 찾아 그 기호를 쓰고, 이유를 서술하시오

_____

_____

11 다음 글을 읽고 아래 물음들에 답하시오.   1-160320

[A] <u>Since</u> you can't use gestures, make faces, or present an object to readers in writing, you must rely on words to do both the telling and the showing. Show more than you tell. Use words to make the reader see. For example, don't leave the reader guessing about Laura's beautiful hair. [B] <u>부드러운 바람이 그녀의 부드러운 갈색 머리 가장자리에 어떻게 닿는지 보여주어라.</u> Don't just say you felt happy. Show yourself leaping down the steps four at a time, coat unzipped, shouting in the wind, "Hurray, I did it!"

아래 보기를 활용하여 [B]에 해당되는 문장을 영작하시오.

```
[보기]
- 총 13단어로 영작할 것.
- show/ brown hair/ silky/ the edge of/ how/
  the gentle wind/ touch를 반드시 사용할 것.
- 필요시 형태나 시제를 변형하여 서술할 것.
```

_____

[A]의 뜻을 서술하시오.

_____

12 다음 글을 읽고 아래 물음에 답하시오.   1-170319

Finally, it was Shaun's turn to give a speech. When he opened his mouth, nothing but air escaped his throat. Then he tried to speak again, not knowing what to say. He had prepared to talk about time and he started with the word: 'Time....' But nothing followed. Shaun could not find the words. Laughter started to pass through the auditorium from front to back. Even the judges looked disappointed. Suddenly, however, His memories were back to him and he could continue his speech. He looked into the crowd. The audience at the contest were laughing out loud now, at him, at his inability.

위 글에서 가장 문법적으로, 혹은 문맥적으로 어색한 문장을 본문에서 찾아 완전한 문장으로 쓰시오.

_____

_____

_____

01 1-180918

Dear Mr. Stevens,

This is a reply to your inquiry about the shipment status of the desk you purchased at our store on September 26. Unfortunately, the delivery of your desk will take longer than expected due to the damage that occurred during the shipment from the furniture manufacturer to our warehouse. We have ordered an exact replacement from the manufacturer, and we expect that delivery will take place within two weeks. As soon as the desk arrives, we will telephone you immediately and arrange a convenient delivery time. We regret the inconvenience this delay has caused you.

Sincerely,

Justin Upton

① 영업시간 변경을 공지하려고
② 고객 서비스 만족도를 조사하려고
③ 상품의 배송 지연에 대해 설명하려고
④ 구매한 상품의 환불 절차를 안내하려고
⑤ 배송된 상품의 파손에 대해 항의하려고

02 1-180919

Garnet blew out the candles and lay down. It was too hot even for a sheet. She lay there, sweating, listening to the empty thunder that brought no rain, and whispered, "I wish the drought would end." Late in the night, Garnet had a feeling that something she had been waiting for was about to happen. She lay quite still, listening. The thunder rumbled again, sounding much louder. And then slowly, one by one, as if someone were dropping pennies on the roof, came the raindrops. Garnet held her breath hopefully. The sound paused. "Don't stop! Please!" she whispered. Then the rain burst strong and loud upon the world. Garnet leaped out of bed and ran to the window. She shouted with joy, "It's raining hard!" She felt as though the thunderstorm was a present.

① wishful → excited   ② embarrassed → proud
③ ashamed → satisfied   ④ indifferent → frightened
⑤ grateful → disappointed

03 1-180920

How do you encourage other people when they are changing their behavior? Suppose you see a friend who is on a diet and has been losing a lot of weight. It's tempting to tell her that she looks great and she must feel wonderful. It feels good for someone to hear positive comments, and this feedback will often be encouraging. However, if you end the discussion there, then the only feedback your friend is getting is about her progress toward an outcome. Instead, continue the discussion. Ask about what she is doing that has allowed her to be successful. What is she eating? Where is she working out? What are the lifestyle changes she has made? When the conversation focuses on the process of change rather than the outcome, it reinforces the value of creating a sustainable process.

① 상대방의 감정을 고려하여 조언해야 한다.
② 토론 중에는 지나치게 공격적인 질문을 삼가야 한다.
③ 효과적인 다이어트를 위해 구체적인 계획을 세워야 한다.
④ 지속적인 성장을 위해서는 단점보다 장점에 집중해야 한다.
⑤ 행동을 바꾸려는 사람과는 과정에 초점을 두어 대화해야 한다.

04 다음 도표의 내용과 일치하지 <u>않는</u> 것은?

1-180924

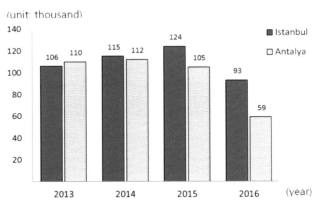

Top Turkish Cities Receiving Tourists

The above graph shows the number of tourists who visited Istanbul and Antalya, the top two most-visited cities in Turkey, from 2013 to 2016. ① The number of tourists to each city was over one hundred thousand every year between 2013 and 2015. ② The city that received the higher number of tourists in 2013 was Antalya, but in the following three years, Istanbul received more tourists than Antalya did. ③ While the number of tourists to Istanbul increased steadily from 2013 to 2015, Antalya received less tourists in 2015 compared to the previous year. ④ Interestingly, in 2016, the number of tourists dropped to less than one hundred thousand for both cities. ⑤ In particular, the number of tourists to Antalya in 2016 was only one-third the number from 2013.

05 Shoes For Schools에 관한 다음 안내문의 내용과 일치하지 <u>않는</u> 것은?

1-180926

SHOES FOR SCHOOLS

Your used shoes can go a long way!

Brooks High School students! Do you have old or unwanted shoes? Donate them for children in Africa. The profits from reselling the shoes will be used to build schools in Africa.

WHAT
* You can give away all types of shoes such as sneakers, sandals, boots, etc.

WHERE
* You can drop shoes off in the collection box on the first floor of the main building.

WHEN
* Between 8:00 a.m. and 4:00 p.m. throughout this semester
* Shoes will be picked up on Tuesdays every two weeks.

HOW
* The shoes you donate need to be in a plastic bag.

For more information, please call 413-367-1391.
Thank you for your participation.

① 모든 수익금은 아프리카에 학교를 짓는 데 쓰인다.
② 모든 종류의 신발을 기증할 수 있다.
③ 신발 수거함은 본관 1층에 있다.
④ 매주 화요일에 신발을 수거한다.
⑤ 기증하는 신발은 비닐봉지에 담겨 있어야 한다.

06 Eddie Adams에 관한 다음 글의 내용과 일치하지 않는 것은?

1-180925

Eddie Adams was born in New Kensington, Pennsylvania. He developed his passion for photography in his teens, when he became a staff photographer for his high school paper. After graduating, he joined the United States Marine Corps, where he captured scenes from the Korean War as a combat photographer. In 1958, he became staff at the Philadelphia Evening Bulletin, a daily evening newspaper published in Philadelphia. In 1962, he joined the Associated Press (AP), and after 10 years, he left the AP to work as a freelancer for Time magazine. The Saigon Execution photo that he took in Vietnam earned him the Pulitzer Prize for Spot News Photography in 1969. He shot more than 350 covers of magazines with portraits of political leaders such as Deng Xiaoping, Richard Nixon, and George Bush.

① 10대 시절에 사진에 대한 열정을 키웠다.
② 종군 사진 기자로 한국전쟁의 장면을 촬영했다.
③ 1962년부터 Time 잡지사에서 일했다.
④ 베트남에서 촬영한 사진으로 퓰리처상을 받았다.
⑤ 정치 지도자들의 잡지 표지용 사진을 촬영했다.

(A)

A 10-year-old boy decided to learn judo despite the fact that he had lost his left arm in a devastating car accident. The boy began lessons with an old Japanese judo master. The boy was doing well, so (a) <u>he</u> couldn't understand why, after three months of training, the master had taught him only one move.

(B)

On the way home, after reviewing all the matches he had, he summoned the courage to ask what was on his mind. "Master, how did I become the champion with only one move?" "You won for two reasons," the master answered. "First, you've mastered one of the most difficult throws in all of judo. And second, the only known defense for that move is for your opponent to grab your left arm." The boy's biggest weakness had become (b) <u>his</u> biggest strength.

(C)

Not quite understanding but believing in his master, the boy kept training. Several months later, the master took the boy to his first tournament. Surprising himself, the boy easily won his first two matches. The third match proved to be more difficult, but after some time, his opponent became impatient and charged; the boy skillfully used his one move to win the match. Still amazed by his success, (c) <u>he</u> was now in the finals.

(D)

This time, his opponent was bigger, stronger, and more experienced. Concerned that (d) <u>he</u> might get hurt, the referee called a timeout to stop the match. Then the master intervened. "No," the master insisted, "let him continue." Soon after the match resumed, his opponent made a critical mistake: (e) <u>he</u> dropped his guard. Instantly, the boy used his move to pin him. The boy had won the match and the tournament. He was the champion.

주어진 글 (A)에 이어질 내용을 순서에 맞게 배열한 것으로 가장 적절한 것은?

① (B) – (D) – (C)
② (C) – (B) – (D)
③ (C) – (D) – (B)
④ (D) – (B) – (C)
⑤ (D) – (C) – (B)

밑줄친 (a)~(e) 중에서 가르키는 대상이 나머지 넷과 <u>다른</u> 것은?

① (a)
② (b)
③ (c)
④ (d)
⑤ (e)

윗글에 관한 내용으로 적절하지 <u>않은</u> 것은?

① 소년은 자동차 사고로 왼팔을 잃었다.
② 소년은 어떻게 자신이 챔피언이 되었는지를 스승에게 물었다.
③ 소년은 유도의 가장 어려운 던지기 동작 중 하나에 통달했다.
④ 소년은 스승을 믿고 훈련을 계속했다.
⑤ 결승전에서 소년의 스승은 타임아웃을 요청했다.

Day 6
p. 38~43

1	⑤	2	④	3	②	4	⑤	5	①
6	②								

Day 6 Assignment
p. 44~49

1	②	2	③	3	⑤	4	⑤	5	④
6	②	7	①	8	⑤	9	⑤	10	②
11	①	12	⑤						

Day 7
p. 52~59

1	④	2	⑤	3	①	4	①	5	③
6	③	7	②	8	d, ②				

Day 7 Assignment
p. 60~66

1	③	2	⑤	3	⑤	4	⑤	5	①
6	①	7	②	8	⑤	9	②	10	①
11	⑤	12	②	13	⑤,① [각각]				

Day 8
p. 68~73

1	④	2	⑤	3	②	4	①	5	①
6	①								

Day 8 Assignment
p. 74~78

1	③	2	②	3	⑤	4	②	5	②
6	④	7	②	8	①	9	①	10	②

Day 9 Assignment
p. 82~87

1	②	2	③	3	③	4	③	5	④
6	④	7	밑 해설 참조	8	밑 해설 참조	9	밑 해설 참조	10	밑 해설 참조
11	밑 해설 참조	12	밑 해설 참조						

Day 10
p. 88~93

1	③	2	①	3	⑤	4	⑤	5	④
6	③	7	③	⑤	⑤				

[7] – the best way to make sure long-term happiness
[8] – We have all met people who limit their lives in the narrowest possible terms
[9] – (모범 답안) 가난한 나라에게 돈을 직접 주게되면 스스로 자립하지 못하고 의존적으로 만들어질 수 있기 때문이다.
[10] – (d) – with > without, (모범 답안) 우리는 집이나 옷 없이 사는 사람 보다 충분히 장난감이나 게임 없이도 잘 살 수 있기 때문이다.
[11] – Show how the gentle wind touches the edge of her silky brown hair, -때문에
[12] – Suddenly, however, His memories were back to him and he could continue his speech.

▮ MEMO

\# 여기까지 온 당신, 과정은 어땠는지 몰라도 확실한건, 당신은 성장했다는 것입니다.